It's My State! ★ ★ ★ ★ ★ ★

NEW JERSEY

The Garden State

David C. King, William McGeveran, and Greg Clinton

Cavendish
Square
New York

Published in 2015 by Cavendish Square Publishing, LLC
243 5th Avenue, Suite 136, New York, NY 10016

Library of Congress Cataloging-in-Publication Data

King, David C.
New Jersey / David King, William McGeveran, Greg Clinton. — Third edition.
pages cm. — (It's my state)
Includes index.
ISBN 978-1-50260-013-4 (hardcover) ISBN 978-1-50260-014-1 (ebook)
1. New Jersey—Juvenile literature. I. McGeveran, William. II. Clinton, Greg. III. Title.

F134.3.K56 2015
974.9—dc23

2014024973

Editor: Fletcher Doyle
Senior Copy Editor: Wendy A. Reynolds
Art Director: Jeffrey Talbot
Designer: Joseph Macri
Senior Production Manager: Jennifer Ryder-Talbot
Production Editor: David McNamara
Photo Research by J8 Media

Printed in the United States of America

NEW JERSEY
CONTENTS

★ State Flower: Purple Violet

Violets bloom across the fields and forests of New Jersey. There are more than five hundred varieties of this delicate flower, many in various shades of purple. In colonial times, violets were widely used as a food and as a base for perfumes.

★ State Tree: Red Oak

The red oak is one of the best-known American hardwoods—woods that are sturdy enough for building houses and flooring. Nearly half the hardwood lumber used in New Jersey comes from its state tree.

★ State Bird: Eastern Goldfinch

Also known as the American goldfinch, the state bird is easy to identify because of the male's bright lemon-yellow body and black cap, wings, and tail. These birds feed on seeds from trees, shrubs, and flowers.

NEW JERSEY

POPULATION: 8,791,894

State Animal: Horse

During the 1700s and much of the 1800s, horses were used to pull carriages, farm and freight wagons, and canal barges and boats. Before steam engines took over, horses even pulled the first railroad cars. The earliest farm machines also depended on horsepower.

State Insect: Honey Bee

In the 1700s and early 1800s, honey was an important agricultural product in New Jersey. The fields of clover in the state's northwest corner were said to produce the best honey. Honey is still big business in the state.

State Dinosaur: Hadrosaurus Foulkii

These duckbilled creatures roamed the swampy lands in what is now New Jersey in the Cretaceous Period, seventy to one hundred million years ago. A fossil of one of these dinosaurs was discovered by William Parke Foulke in Haddonfield in 1858. It became the state dinosaur in 1991.

Mountain Laurels are among the many
flowering plants that give New Jersey
its nickname.

The Garden State

People who visit or pass through New Jersey sometimes wonder why it is called the Garden State. Along busy stretches of the New Jersey **Turnpike**, past big cities such as Newark, there seem to be more smokestacks than trees, more warehouses than gardens. The confusion about the nickname is understandable. The land area of New Jersey is only 7,417 square miles (19,210 square kilometers). Only three states are smaller. Yet as of 2010, New Jersey had a population of close to nine million people—the eleventh largest of any state. New Jersey has about 1,200 people for each square mile of land (460 per sq. km), making it the most densely populated state in the country.

However, the population is concentrated in the northeast. A short drive in any direction can take you to a hilly semi-wilderness, where clear streams sparkle beneath towering oaks and maples. Not far to the south is a vast region called the Pine Barrens, where cranberry bogs give way to one of the largest forested areas on the mid-Atlantic Coast.

New Jersey has twenty-one counties. The most crowded is Hudson County, which lies across the Hudson River from New York City. The county has more than 14,000 people per square mile (5,600 per sq. km). On the other hand, Salem County, in the southwest, has only about two hundred people per square mile (fewer than eighty people per sq. km).

The state includes four natural land regions. The Piedmont is a belt of raised land that extends from the northeastern border with New York southwest across New Jersey. From there, the Piedmont stretches as far south as Alabama. The Highlands region of New Jersey, located northwest of the Piedmont, is a narrow strip of steep hills and valleys. In the state's far northwest corner is the Appalachian Ridge and Valley region. The bottom three-fifths of the state lies within the Atlantic Coastal Plain.

New Jersey Borders	
North:	New York
South:	Delaware Bay
East:	New York Atlantic Ocean
West:	Pennsylvania Delaware

The Piedmont

In the northeast corner of New Jersey, the Hudson River separates the state from New York's Westchester County and from the towering skyscrapers of New York City. This geographic region is an area of gentle hills that is about 200 feet (60 meters) above sea level. The Piedmont covers only about one-fifth of the state's land area. More than half the state's people live there, especially in the eastern part. Four of New Jersey's six largest cities are located in the Piedmont: Newark, Jersey City, Paterson, and Elizabeth.

The Palisades line the western side of the Hudson River.

One of New Jersey's many pleasant natural surprises is a region of cliffs called the Palisades. Rising from 300 to 550 feet (90 to 170 m) above the Hudson River, these sheer cliffs extend north from Hoboken, New Jersey, to Nyack, New York, on the river's west bank. They were formed close to 200 million years ago. At the time, molten lava rose from deep in the earth's crust and hardened. Today, this dramatic wall of gray-black rock with streaks of dark red adds to the beauty of the region around the Hudson River.

Another unique feature of the Piedmont is an area called the Great Swamp National Wildlife Refuge. These wetlands were created more than ten thousand years ago, during the last ice age, when the movement of glaciers carved up the land. The area, within sight of New York City's skyscrapers, was at one point chosen as the site for a new airport. But New Jersey residents protested, and in 1960, the swamp was set aside as a wildlife refuge. Today, it is home to nearly one thousand plant and animal species, including more than two hundred bird species alone. Several miles of trails and boardwalks make it a user-friendly sanctuary.

The decline of manufacturing industries in recent years affected some parts of the Piedmont. For example, the Hudson River waterfront became littered with rotting piers and crumbling warehouses that had been abandoned for decades. Since the late 1990s, however, the state has made efforts to repair the region. Broken-down structures have been replaced by attractive apartment complexes, row houses, and modern office buildings.

High Point Monument, built in the 1930s in the Kittatinny Mountains to honor war veterans, marks the highest spot in New Jersey.

NEW JERSEY
COUNTY MAP

SUSSEX

PASSAIC

BERGEN

WARREN

MORRIS

ESSEX

HUDSON

UNION

HUNTERDON

SOMERSET

MIDDLESEX

MERCER

MONMOUTH

BURLINGTON

OCEAN

CAMDEN

GLOUCESTER

SALEM

ATLANTIC

CUMBERLAND

CAPE MAY

NEW JERSEY
POPULATION BY COUNTY

County	Population	County	Population	County	Population
Atlantic	274,549	Hunterdon	128,349	Sussex	149,265
Bergen	905,116	Mercer	366,513	Union	536,499
Burlington	448,734	Middlesex	809,858	Warren	108,692
Camden	513,657	Monmouth	630,380		
Cape May	97,265	Morris	492,276		
Cumberland	156,898	Ocean	576,567		
Essex	783,969	Passaic	501,226		
Gloucester	288,288	Salem	66,083		
Hudson	634,266	Somerset	323,444		

Source: U.S. Bureau of the Census, 2010

The New York City skyline is visible from the Meadowlands

The Highlands

A short drive to the west of New Jersey's bustling cities and nearby suburbs will take travelers to the Highlands region. This is a semi-wilderness area that covers nearly 1,000 square miles (2,600 sq. km) of steep hills and narrow valleys. Many of the state's eight hundred lakes and ponds are located there and provide scenic recreation areas for both residents and tourists. The Highlands region is also a vital **watershed**. It supplies water to millions of New Jerseyans living to the east.

The Appalachian Valley and Ridge Region

The smallest of New Jersey's land regions is located in the far northwest. The Appalachian Valley and Ridge is part of the large Appalachian Mountain chain, which stretches from the Saint Lawrence River in Canada to Georgia in the south. Part of the Appalachian Trail cuts through New Jersey in this region. The trail crosses the Kittatinny Mountains, the largest mountains in the state. The state's tallest peak reaches 1,803 feet (550 m) high. Its name is fitting: High Point.

The hills in this region may not be very tall, but they are steep. This gives them a rugged appearance. The grassy valleys and hills are perfect for apple orchards and herds of dairy cattle.

The Delaware Water Gap is one of New Jersey's most popular vacation areas.

The Delaware Water Gap forms the border between northwestern New Jersey and Pennsylvania. The famous Delaware Water Gap National Recreation Area straddles about 40 miles (65 km) of the Delaware River. This is one of the most popular scenic areas in the eastern United States. It draws about five million visitors each year.

The Atlantic Coastal Plain and Southern New Jersey

An invisible line runs northeast across the state, from Trenton, the state capital, to the Atlantic Coast at Perth Amboy. This is called the fall line. It is marked by waterfalls and rapids on the Raritan River and other flowing bodies of water.

The region south and east of this fall line is part of the Atlantic Coastal Plain. This region begins on Cape Cod in Massachusetts and extends down the eastern seaboard to Georgia. The Atlantic Coastal Plain covers about 60 percent of New Jersey's land area, but holds only about one-fourth of the population.

When most people in New Jersey mention southern New Jersey, they are referring to the state's Atlantic coastline, which they call "the Shore." This part of the Atlantic Coastal Plain is a long stretch of sandy beaches and barrier islands. The islands are long, narrow sandbars separated by tidal inlets (small waterways) and lagoons. Many of the islands are family-oriented resort communities. Others have nature sanctuaries. In geographic terms, the Jersey Shore is the Outer Coastal Plain. The Inner Coastal Plain is much larger and slightly elevated, though it rarely gets more than 100 feet (30 m) above sea level.

Horse farms dot the state's large Coastal Plain region.

Atlantic City

Cape May lighthouse

Edison's Menlo Park lab

1. Atlantic City

Park Place! Boardwalk! Atlantic City is the inspiration for the original version of the game Monopoly. Best known for casinos and gambling, Atlantic City (during **Prohibition** in the 1920s) is the setting of the hit HBO show *Boardwalk Empire*.

2. Cape May

The tiny seaside town of Cape May, at the very southern tip of the state, is a famous resort destination. It is the oldest seaside resort in the country, and attracts visitors with beautiful Victorian buildings, fantastic beaches, and great bird-watching opportunities.

3. Delaware Water Gap

This 70,000-acre (28,328 hectares) park on the border of Pennsylvania provides access to kayaking, canoeing, hiking, fishing, rock climbing, and more. Among the hikes is a trail that will take you to Kittatinny Ridge, the highest spot in the state.

4. Liberty State Park

Situated on the water across the Hudson River from Lower Manhattan, Liberty State Park is a 1,200 acre (486 ha) park that contains the Liberty Walkway, ferry rides to the Statue of Liberty and Ellis Island, and the Liberty Science Center.

5. Menlo Park

The inventor Thomas Edison created some of his most important inventions at a laboratory in New Jersey, earning him the nickname "The Wizard of Menlo Park." The site of his lab is now in a state park, with a museum dedicated to Edison's life and work.

6. New Jersey State Museum

Located in Trenton, the New Jersey State Museum houses the state archives, as well as an impressive collection of art and archaeological artifacts.

7. Ocean City

Ocean City is one of the country's best beach destinations. In the summer, the town's population jumps from eleven thousand to more than 120,000! Ocean City attracts families with its range of kid-friendly parks and entertainment and its law banning the sale of alcohol.

8. Palisades Interstate Park

This is a chain of twenty-four parks and eight historic sites along the west bank of the Hudson River. Millions of visitors enjoy its more than 100,000 acres (40,468 Ha) of natural beauty each year.

9. Princeton Art Museum

Princeton University is one of the most prestigious places of higher education in the world. Its art museum, free to the public, houses a massive collection of important works of art, from African, Ancient American, and European and Contemporary Art.

10. Statue of Liberty and Ellis Island

While the Statue of Liberty and Ellis Island are inside the New Jersey borders, these national monuments are actually administered by New York State. (It is the only case in which one state controls land that is inside another state.)

New Jersey State Museum

Palisades Interstate Park

Statue of Liberty

Pakim Pond is one of many beautiful spots in the Pinelands National Reserve.

Near the fall line, the Inner Coastal Plain has suburbs and small towns, many dating back to the early 1700s. Campuses for two of the state's best-known universities—Princeton and Rutgers—are located there. The soil is excellent for farming. The northern area of the Coastal Plain has many farms that specialize in tomatoes and other vegetables, including an increasing variety of unusual vegetables from Asia.

The largest area of southern New Jersey's Coastal Plain is a 2,000-square-mile (5,200 sq. km) area called the Pine Barrens, or Pinelands. The soil is not useful for ordinary farming. However, the wetland regions are ideal for cranberry bogs, and some drier areas have been turned into blueberry farms. Most of the area is under government protection as the Pinelands National Reserve. The area is home to dozens of rare plant and animal species, including plant varieties that are normally found farther south. Plants that thrive there include pitcher plants and several kinds of bladderworts. These plants are known as "meat eaters" because they trap and digest insects. The Pine Barrens also contains rare species of frogs, turtles, and snakes.

The beautiful Pine Barrens Tree Frog likes the white cedar swamps and peat moss of the Pine Barrens. This frog is regarded as a symbol of the Pinelands. It was once considered endangered, but it has done well in recent years. In 2007, the state government upgraded its status from endangered (at risk of dying out) to threatened (at risk of becoming endangered in the near future). A new threat to the tree frog was spotted in the summer of 2014. A study found that development near the Pine Barrens was affecting the water supply, causing pH levels (a measure of acidity or alkalinity of liquids) in the water to rise. The tree frog, and much of the plant life in the Pine Barrens, requires a low pH level of 3.5 to 5.5. Numbers below 7 indicate acidity and numbers above 7 alkalinity. When acid levels decrease, other species move in and push out native species such as the Pine Barren Tree Frog.

Cape May lies at the southern tip of New Jersey. From Cape May, the Jersey Shore extends northward along some 130 miles (200 km) of beaches and coastal islands. Fifty resort cities and towns, including Atlantic City, draw vacationers in the summer. Sandy Hook, in the north, is a 6.5-mile-long (10.5 km) peninsula that stretches into the Atlantic Ocean. Black cherry trees and ancient holly trees provide food for migrating birds. This sandy area is said to be the best place in the nation to observe migrating hawks.

Climate

New Jersey measures only 167 miles (269 km) north to south and 56 miles (90 km) wide. Despite the state's small size, its climate varies from one region to another. The coldest areas are in the northwest corner. The average January temperature there is about 28 degrees Fahrenheit (−2 degrees Celsius), and summers are cool because of the higher altitude. In the southwest, the winter temperature is about 34°F (1°C). Summers are quite warm, averaging 76°F (24°C) in July. The ocean keeps coastal temperatures warmer during winter and cooler in the summer. However, the long, low coastline is

Winters are cold enough to allow skating on Lake Carnegie in Princeton.

sometimes hit by hurricanes and strong winter storms called nor'easters, which sweep in off the Atlantic.

Northern New Jersey gets 40 to 50 inches (101 to 127 centimeters) of snow each year. The southernmost parts of the state get only 10 to 15 inches (25 to 38 cm). The snow can create dangerous driving conditions. However, skiing and snowboarding are favorite winter pastimes for many New Jerseyans, and the icy lakes and ponds are ideal for ice skating and hockey.

Wild New Jersey

The varied landscapes and climate make New Jersey an ideal place for a wide range of plant and animal life. The state boasts nearly fifty state parks and forests. There are also more than one hundred special so-called wildlife management areas. These protected areas offer people a chance to view wildlife sanctuaries from roads, trails, and boardwalks, sometimes within the shadow of high-rise apartments and office buildings.

Beech, cedar, maple, poplar, birch, and oak trees are found across the state. In the fall, leaves change color, turning the landscape into a lovely blend of orange, red, and yellow. In the spring, summer, and fall, flowers bloom across all parts of the state. Flowering plants such as buttercups, azaleas, bloodroot, mountain laurels, and lilies are native to the state. New Jersey's trees, shrubs, and flowers provide both food and homes for wildlife.

Much of New Jersey's wildlife lives in the woodlands found across the state. Most of the animals common to the northeastern United States are found there. These include

Hiking the woodland trails is popular in the Forsythe National Wildlife Refuge.

The Cape May Bird Observatory delights thousands of bird-watchers.

white-tailed deer, raccoons, opossums, red foxes, coyotes, squirrels, skunks, and rabbits. Porcupines, beavers, and bats also make New Jersey their home. Smaller numbers of black bears and bobcats continue to prowl the heavily wooded hillsides.

New Jersey is also known for its number and variety of birds. The state is on the Atlantic Flyway. This is the route that migrating birds take to their nesting grounds in Central and South America. In addition, the state's mild climate and many sanctuaries and wilderness areas create ideal conditions for nesting. Cape May might be the most famous location in the country for bird-watchers. More than 100,000 bird-watchers visit the area every year, and hundreds of species of birds have been seen there.

The many lakes, ponds, streams, and rivers also provide homes to New Jersey wildlife. Fish such as bass, trout, and pike swim through the waters. Lobsters, crabs, oysters, and clams live in the state's coastal waters. Sometimes whales can be seen moving through the ocean. Ducks, geese, egrets, herons, and pelicans are among the many birds that can be seen wading and swimming in or flying above the state's waterways.

New Jersey is a mixture of rolling hills, sandy beaches, numerous waterways, and dramatic landscapes. The variety of land and water—and diverse plant and animal life—helps make the Garden State a pleasant place that its people are proud to call home.

10 KEY PLANTS AND ANIMALS

Bald Eagle

Opossum

Pine Barrens Tree Frog

1. Bald Eagle

During the 1970s and 1980s the bald eagle, the national symbol of the United States, was endangered in New Jersey; there was only a single pair of nesting eagles in the state during this time. Conservation efforts increased the nesting eagle pairs to 119 in 2012.

2. Box Turtle

The box turtle can be found throughout the state. They are called "box" turtles because they can retract their bodies into their shells and close the shell tight using a kind of "hinge," like a box closing. These creatures can live more than one hundred years.

3. Opossum

The opossum's strong tail enables the animal to hang upside down. When trapped on the ground, the opossum may fake being dead until the danger is over. That is where the term "playing possum" comes from.

4. Orchid

The wetlands of New Jersey's Pine Barrens are home to about twenty species of orchids. Many of these varieties are normally found much farther south.

5. Pine Barrens Tree Frog

This beautiful green, purple, white, and yellow tree frog measures only 1 to 2 inches long (2.2 to 4.4 cm). It uses swamps or ponds to breed, and makes its home in special forests of cedar, pine, and those with thick moss cover.

6. Piping Plover

Plovers nest on the ground, so their eggs and offspring are in danger from humans and animals. These birds began declining in numbers in the late 1940s, as beaches became more developed. Conservation efforts have helped reverse the decline, but plovers are still considered threatened in New Jersey.

7. Prickly Pear

Along the Delaware Water Gap, the hillsides form natural rock gardens that erupt in bright yellow blossoms of the prickly pear—a cactus often associated with the Southwest. When the blossoms fade, the cacti produce the purple-pink "pear."

8. Red Fox

The red fox lost much of its habitat as cities and suburbs spread across the state. However, these intelligent little animals are still a common sight in the hills of northwestern New Jersey, in the Highlands region, and in the Pine Barrens.

9. Timber Rattlesnake

Once a very successful species in New Jersey, timber rattlesnake habitats in the north of the state have been destroyed or limited, and people kill these venomous snakes when they see them, reducing the population.

10. Warbler

Southern New Jersey is famous for bird watching. The many varieties of nesting warblers are especially exciting for bird watchers. These include yellow-throated, pine, prairie, blue-winged, worm-eating, black-and-white, and Cape May warblers.

Piping Plover

Prickly Pear

Red Fox

Important Revolutionary War battles were fought in New Jersey.

From the Beginning

New Jersey sits on land that is bordered by rich river and ocean resources, mountains, flatlands and swamps, and land fit for orchards and agriculture. The state's history, especially before the rise of New York City and the global shipping industry, can be seen as the story of how to best manage these resources.

The First People

Little is known about the first people who lived in present-day New Jersey. The earliest groups probably arrived in the region about ten thousand years ago. By the year 1600, New Jersey was home to the Lenape people. They hunted, fished, and gathered wild plant foods. They also planted crops, such as beans, squash, corn, and tobacco. They lived in small communities, sometimes built along riverbanks. Their homes, called *wigwams*, were made out of saplings, bark, and other plant material. The wigwams were small and usually round, though they could be long or oblong (these larger structures were called longhouses). The Lenape used materials such as animal hides, seashells, plants, and clay to make their own clothes, baskets, and pottery. Some Lenape also made swift canoes out of bark and other tree parts.

Today, the original Lenape people would hardly recognize the homeland they once called "Scheyichbi," or, "the place bordering the ocean." Yet many place names in modern

New Jersey come from their language. For example, the town of Absecon gets its name from a Lenape word meaning "place of swans." Manhattan (in New York) is a name derived from a Lenape word for "island of many hills." Hoboken, the name of a city in New Jersey on the Hudson River, is Lenape for "place where pipes are traded," and the Pessaic River is named for the Lenape word for "river that flows through a valley."

Europeans Arrive

The first European explorer to land on the shore of present-day New Jersey was Giovanni da Verrazzano, an Italian sea captain who sailed for France in 1524. Verrazzano, however, did not claim the land for France. Nearly a century passed before Europeans settled in this part of North America.

In 1609, Henry Hudson sailed along the New Jersey coast before entering the river that now bears his name. Hudson was an English explorer who sailed under the flag of the Netherlands. He claimed the area for the Dutch. By 1630, about two hundred Dutch fur trappers and traders had settled along the Atlantic Coast. They soon had rivals in the area—Swedish colonists, who settled in present-day Wilmington, Delaware, in 1638.

Henry Hudson met with Native Americans along the river that bears his name.

Early governments weren't always kind to the Quakers, who built this meetinghouse in Burlington in 1683.

The Dutch forced the Swedish colonists to surrender in 1655 and ruled the area as part of their colony of New Netherland. The colony included the town called New Amsterdam at the southern end of Manhattan Island in what is now New York City. It also included other settlements in what is now New York State. By 1660, it also included the settlement that later became Jersey City.

Soon a more powerful rival—England—claimed modern-day New Jersey and the surrounding area as its own. King Charles II of England granted the area to his brother, the Duke of York. In 1664, an English fleet sailed into the harbor of New Amsterdam and demanded the surrender of all of New Netherland. The Dutch governor, Peter Stuyvesant, wanted to defend the colony, but the settlers would not support him. Stuyvesant surrendered without a fight. The English renamed the captured Dutch colony New York.

The Duke of York gave the area between the Hudson and Delaware rivers to two friends. One of them, Sir George Carteret, had been governor of the island of Jersey in the English Channel. The new colony was named New Jersey in his honor. Carteret and his friend Lord John Berkeley attracted hundreds of colonists by offering land at very low cost. They also allowed religious freedom and gave people a voice in the government. However, the government was sometimes hostile to certain religious groups, such as Quakers. From 1674 to 1702, New Jersey was divided into East and West Jersey, with separate capitals. In 1702, England reunited the colony. However, the two capitals remained until 1775, one at Perth Amboy, the other at Burlington.

The Native People

The area of modern New Jersey was originally the home of the Lenape, which in their language meant simply "man." Early European settlers called them the Delaware Indians. The Lenape were a branch of the Algonquian family of tribes. The Algonquian were among the first Native Peoples to meet the European explorers who landed on the Atlantic Coast during the 1500s and 1600s.

The Lenape were really a group of tribes that all spoke dialects of the same language. Young men married outside their clan, and the children they and their new wives had belonged to the mother's clan. This **matrilineal** structure was confusing to the first European explorers. In Europe, children are named for their fathers, and family names are passed down through sons. The Lenape, whose clans included the Lenni-Lenape, the Nanticoke, and the Munsee, were sophisticated farmers and fishermen, and had developed relatively big fishing operations and revolving agriculture. They moved from settlement to settlement, in a kind of revolving circuit called **agricultural shifting**, as the seasons for planting, or harvesting clams, or hunting arrived. The Lenape moved less frequently than other Native tribes further west, and they inhabited permanent structures much of the time, rather than tepees or tents.

As European settlement increased, the Delaware were forced off their land. Expansion displaced most Native Americans in the area during the 1700s, pushing them south and west. These tribes are not extinct, but except for the descendants of New Jersey Native American people who hid or assimilated into white society, they do not live in New Jersey anymore. Most tribes that once were native to New Jersey ended up on reservations in Oklahoma.

There are no federally recognized tribes in New Jersey. The Nanticoke Lenni-Lenape Indians of New Jersey, the Ramapough Lenape Nation, and the Powhatan Renape Indians, have been recognized in the state by statutes but have not received official recognition by New Jersey.

Spotlight on the Lenape

Lenape tribes occupied land stretching from the Delaware Bay at the south end of New Jersey to eastern Pennsylvania and southern New York.

Clans: The Lenape group of First Peoples was made up of various clans divided by language dialects, including the Lenni-Lenape, Nanticoke, and Munsee.

Lenape longhouses could shelter several families.

Homes: Lenape families and clans lived in wigwams or longhouses. Wigwams were small houses for a single family, framed with saplings and covered in mats made of bark or woven cloth. Longhouses could shelter several families at a time. This architecture was more permanent than the lean-tos and tepees of other Native traditions.

Food and Agriculture: The Lenape were relatively **sedentary**; they had developed advanced farming and fishing techniques, so they didn't need to be as **nomadic** as other tribes, and they could support a larger population. They harvested clams in southern New Jersey, farmed corn and beans, and caught large numbers of fish in the rivers of the Delaware region.

Clothing: The men wore loincloths or simple leggings, and the women made elaborate and beautiful winter cloaks. Both men and women wore fur from bears or beavers to keep warm in the winter.

Tools: Hunting was done with bows and arrows. Warriors carried heavy wooden war clubs and body-length shields of moose hide and wood.

The Colonial Years

Throughout the 1700s, New Jersey prospered as a farming colony. Efforts to establish a whaling port in the south were unsuccessful, and business developed slowly. Some colonists thought that New Jersey was doomed to be dominated by the two large cities nearby—Philadelphia to the west and New York to the east. One New Jersey merchant said, "Our wealth ends up in those cities. We are becoming like a keg tapped at both ends."

The people of New Jersey, however, soon found that their location between the two big cities could be a source of strength. As colonial America grew and became prosperous, New Jersey was in a crucial position for moving goods and people between New York and Philadelphia. In the early 1700s, colonial America's first **stagecoach** service was established across New Jersey to connect the two cities. That was just the beginning. From then on, New Jersey's role as a go-between for Philadelphia and New York steadily expanded.

In Their Own Words

"All our hopes were blasted by that unhappy affair at Trenton."

—British government official Lord Germain, on the British defeat at the Battle of Trenton

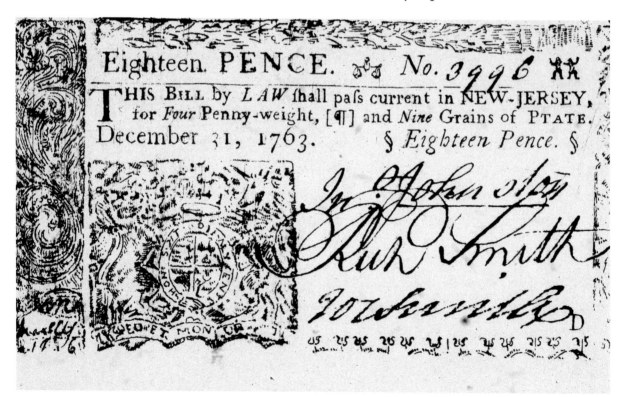

This 18-pence note is now a collector's item.

George Washington's Christmas night crossing of the Delaware River into New Jersey in 1776 preceded a victory for his army at Trenton.

The American Revolution

From 1754 to 1763, Great Britain (which had been formed by the union of England and Scotland) fought against France for control of eastern North America. The conflict was known as the French and Indian War. Britain defeated France, but the cost of the war put the British government deeply in debt. As a result, Great Britain tried to tighten its control over trade with its thirteen American colonies and imposed new taxes on the colonies. Many colonists, known as patriots, believed they were too heavily taxed and were not given a fair say in how they were governed.

In 1774, patriots in Greenwich in southwestern New Jersey borrowed an idea from the Boston Tea Party. They protested the British tax on tea by burning a shipload of British tea. The following year, problems between the colonies and Great Britain turned into war. Early fighting broke out at Lexington and Concord in Massachusetts. On July 4, 1776, representatives of the colonies approved the Declaration of Independence. The famous document stated that the colonies now considered themselves free of British rule. The Declaration of Independence was an important step toward making the Thirteen Colonies into one united, independent nation.

The fight against Britain for independence, the American Revolution, lasted from 1775 to 1783. During the war, thousands of New Jerseyans joined the colonies' Continental Army, led by General George Washington. However, other New Jerseyans, who called themselves

Making A Wigwam

Wigwams are small semi-permanent structures used by the Lenape people as homes for a single family. They were shaped like a dome, built using slender logs bent into a semi-circle, and secured with rope. They were then covered with hides, cloth, grass, or brush. You can make a model of a wigwam using corkboard, sticks, and other easy to find items.

What You Need

10 or 12 straight, flexible sticks
String
Paper
Compass
1 cork board
Glue or tape

What to Do

- Use the compass to draw a circle on the corkboard. This marks the base of your structure.

- Have an adult drill 8–10 evenly spaced holes (each hole should have another hole directly opposite it) around this circle, making sure not to drill entirely through the board.

- Tie two or three sticks together lengthwise using the pieces of string to make four (eight holes) or five (ten holes) rods of about the same length. Insert the rods into two holes opposite each other, bending them to make the domed roof. Use glue to keep the ends of the rods in the drilled holes.

- Tie or glue the rods together where they intersect. Cut your paper into strips, and then cut thin "fringes" into each strip. Attach the strips to your frame using glue or tape. Make sure you leave space for the door.

You should now have a working wigwam model!

You can tie together sticks for your wigwam two at a time or all at once.

loyalists, wanted to stay under British rule. Some loyalists left their homes in New Jersey to move to areas protected by the British. The governor of New Jersey, William Franklin, was among the loyalists who left. He was the son of Benjamin Franklin, one of the leading patriots and Founding Fathers of the new nation.

New Jersey's location made it a natural battleground. Both sides wanted control of the Hudson and Delaware rivers. Nearly a hundred armed clashes took place in New Jersey, including three major battles: Trenton, Princeton, and Monmouth.

The Battle of Trenton is often regarded as the conflict that saved the patriot cause in its darkest hour. In the autumn of 1776, Washington's Continental Army had been badly beaten by a powerful British force. After losing New York City and Long Island to the British, Washington and his battered troops retreated. They moved west through New Jersey, crossing the Delaware River into Pennsylvania. By late December, the patriot cause seemed hopeless. Washington's once-proud army of twenty-five thousand now numbered fewer than four thousand. Many did not have winter coats or shoes.

On December 25—Christmas night—Washington led his men back across the ice-clogged Delaware River. At dawn, they surprised a regiment of German troops hired by the British, and won a stunning victory in the Battle of Trenton. A few days later, Washington struck again, defeating the British at the Battle of Princeton. Those two victories gave patriot troops much-needed confidence to keep fighting.

In June 1778, Washington's army fought the British at the Battle of Monmouth. Neither side could claim victory in the battle, but the British were forced to withdraw. The battle showed that the Continental Army could hold its own against the mighty British. Monmouth marked the last time during the American Revolution that two major armies met in battle in New Jersey. However, the two sides fought many smaller battles over the next few years. Life remained difficult for Washington's army. The winter of 1779–1780 is said to have been the coldest of the century. At their camp in Morristown, New Jersey, Washington's men suffered severely from hunger and cold. About a hundred died from the extreme weather.

In Their Own Words

"... as the sword was the last resort for the preservation of our liberties, so it ought to be the first thing laid aside, when those liberties are firmly established."

—George Washington, in a letter to Congress one week after the Battle of Trenton

General George Washington set up his winter headquarters in 1779-80 at this mansion in Morristown.

The war officially ended with the signing of the Treaty of Paris in September 1783. Great Britain recognized the independence of the newly formed United States. The last British troops left American soil a few months later.

One of the most famous legends of the American Revolution grew out of the Battle of Monmouth. It is said that a heroic wife carried pitchers of water to her husband's unit. When her husband collapsed, the woman helped work one of the cannons for the rest of the battle. She was later called Molly Pitcher. In fact, her true identity is not completely certain, and some historians doubt that she even existed.

A New Nation

In the summer of 1787, delegates from twelve of the thirteen former colonies—now states—met at the Constitutional Convention in Philadelphia. (Only Rhode Island did not send any representatives.) The delegates hoped to create a constitution that provided for a strong national government while also protecting the rights of the individual states. At the convention, New Jersey's William Paterson proposed a single-chamber legislature, or lawmaking body. In Paterson's plan, each state—even a small state such as New Jersey—would have the same number of representatives. His plan was not accepted, but it did contribute to the Great Compromise. This plan created a U.S. Congress with two houses. States with larger populations would have more members in the House of Representatives. But in the Senate, each state would have two senators, regardless of its population. On December 18, 1787, New Jersey ratified, or approved, the U.S. Constitution. By doing so, it became the third state to officially join the United States. In 1790, Trenton was chosen as the new state capital.

New Business and Technology

New Jersey grew and expanded with the other states of the new nation. Agriculture continued to flourish, and transportation and industry became more important. Alexander Hamilton, who served as the first U.S. secretary of the Treasury, planned a model industrial city. The city of Paterson was built at the Great Falls of the Passaic River. The water from the falls was used to create power for nearby factories. These factories used newly developed machines that produced goods quickly and at a low cost. Some of these goods included textiles, tools, and weapons.

In 1804, John Stevens from Hoboken developed a twin-propeller steamboat. In 1811, he launched the nation's first steamboat ferry service, between Hoboken and New York City. In 1825, Stevens created a "steam waggon," which ran on an iron track around his estate. This experiment helped prove that steam railroads were possible. His son, Robert Stevens, started the country's first steam railroad line in 1831. The Camden and Amboy Railroad used a British locomotive called *John Bull*. The railroad line strengthened the economic ties between New York and Philadelphia. The famous Stevens Institute of Technology, in Hoboken, is named after the family that contributed so much to the development of the state.

Running water from the Passaic River powered factories in Paterson.

10 KEY CITIES

Newark Airport

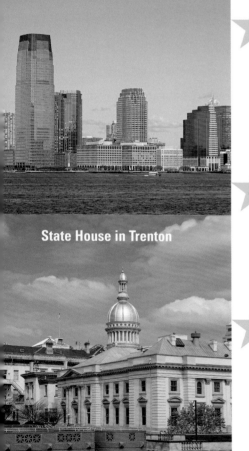

Jersey City

State House in Trenton

1. Newark: population 277,140

The largest city in New Jersey, Newark is a major shipping and transportation hub for the East Coast. Newark Liberty International Airport is one of three key airports that service the larger New York Metropolitan area.

2. Jersey City: population 247,597

Part of the New York metro region, located across the Hudson River from New York City, Jersey City is one of the most ethnically diverse cities in the world. It also has, among U.S. cities, one of the highest percentages of residents who work as artists.

3. Paterson: population 146,199

Formerly known as the "Silk City" due to the role it played in late nineteenth-century silk production, Paterson has been featured in works by poets William Carlos Williams and Allen Ginsberg, in several of Junot Diaz's novels, and in the hit TV show *The Sopranos*.

4. Elizabeth: population 124,969

Restaurants, shops, and parks abound in this lively small city, named by Popular Science magazine as one of "America's 50 Greenest Cities." Parts of Newark airport are in Elizabeth, as well as the Port Newark-Elizabeth Marine Terminal.

5. Trenton: population 84,913

Trenton is the capital of New Jersey, and the state is the largest employer in the city. Nearly 20,000 government employees commute into the city each workday. Trenton's famous landmarks include a monument to George Washington's 1776 victory against Hessian forces during the American Revolution.

NEW JERSEY

6. Clifton: population 84,136

A small city in Pessaic County, Clifton is home to colorful New Jersey landmarks such as Rutt's Hut (a deep-fried hot dog restaurant) and a number of locations where episodes for *The Sopranos* were filmed.

7. Camden: population 77,344

Just across the Delaware River from Pennsylvania, Camden is the location of Campbell Soup Company headquarters and a number of medical and educational institutions. In recent decades Camden has struggled with poverty, unemployment, and crime.

8. Passaic: population 69,781

The neighbor of Clifton, Passaic has some architecturally interesting homes and churches. It houses a significant Orthodox Jewish population.

9. Union City: population 66,455

West of Hoboken, Union City has been called "Havana on the Hudson" because of its significant Cuban population. The annual Cuban Day Parade draws crowds, and the city also hosts artistic and cultural events, such as the Union City International Film Festival.

10. East Orange: population 64,270

The hometown of Queen Latifah, East Orange is conveniently located near the New York metropolitan area and Newark Liberty International Airport.

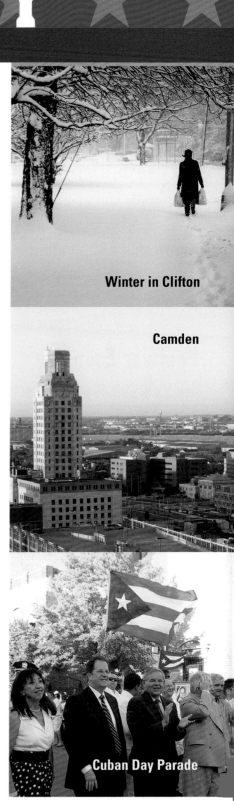

Winter in Clifton

Camden

Cuban Day Parade

The Civil War

During the 1800s, the issue of slavery divided the United States. The plantations in Southern states depended on slaves to work the fields. Northern states, including New Jersey, relied on smaller farms and on industries in which slave labor did not provide a big advantage. Many Northerners also believed that slavery was morally wrong. In 1804, New Jersey voted for gradual emancipation of slaves in the state. Lawmakers decided that all males born into slavery would become free at age twenty-five, and females would become free at age twenty-one. Tensions between the North and South continued to grow and led to the Civil War (1861–1865). Eleven Southern states seceded from, or left, the Union (that is, the United States) and formed the Confederate States of America.

During the Civil War, more than eighty thousand young men from New Jersey wore the dark blue uniforms of the Union army. Some people in New Jersey sided with the Confederacy, but the state as a whole remained loyal to the Union. After years of bloody battles, the Union won the war in 1865. In December of that year, the Thirteenth Amendment to the U.S. Constitution officially ended slavery throughout the United States.

Postwar Economy

The economy of New Jersey continued to grow. Silk processing and other industries were developed in Paterson. Oil production became important in Bayonne, and Camden became a center for shipbuilding.

Women weave silk at a time when New Jersey was a center for the textile industry.

The period from the 1860s to the 1890s was known as the Age of the Robber Barons. The robber barons were powerful business leaders such as John D. Rockefeller, who made a fortune in the oil industry, and Andrew Carnegie, who did the same in the steel industry. They accumulated great wealth by creating **monopolies** in their fields. A monopoly is a company that controls so much of an industry that it has no competition and can charge high prices for its goods or services.

Building Better Bridges

John Roebling opened a factory in Trenton, New Jersey in 1848 to meet demand for his wire rope. Roebling and his two sons, Washington and Ferdinand, built a suspension bridge across the gorge of the Niagara River. They then built the Brooklyn Bridge as well as many other suspension bridges in the United States.

New Jersey politicians saw the rise of these powerful companies as a great opportunity. The state legislature passed laws that encouraged big corporations to set up offices in New Jersey. Monopolies were illegal in other states, but New Jersey allowed them. By the late 1800s, roughly half the nation's largest corporations had established headquarters in New Jersey.

The 1900s and Beyond

The American people became upset with the spread of monopolies. In the early 1900s, President Theodore Roosevelt and other reformers worked to break up these powerful companies. In New Jersey, the reform leader was Woodrow Wilson. He served first as president of Princeton University and then as governor of New Jersey. Wilson was elected president of the United States in 1912 and 1916. In 1917, he led the nation into World War I.

New Jersey played an important role during World War I and World War II, which the United States entered in 1941. Hundreds of thousands of troops trained

Woodrow Wilson (left) casting his vote in 1912.

Orson Welles stirred the populace with his radio broadcast of "The War of the Worlds."

and gathered at Camp Dix (later Fort Dix) and other facilities in the state before heading off to war. The state's industries produced wartime products, including chemicals, weapons, ships, and aircraft engines. New Jersey also became a leader in military research and technology.

The most notorious media event of all time occurred between the World Wars. On October 30, 1938, actor-director Orson Welles broadcast a radio drama that sounded like a real news broadcast. "The War of the Worlds" described a landing by Martians on a farm near the New Jersey town of Grover's Mill. Thousands of listeners missed the on-air warnings that the invasion was made up, and some panicked.

The size of the panic is in dispute. There were reports of thousands of New Jersey residents jamming highways in an attempt to flee from the Martians. Some people now believe these reports were exaggerated by newspapers, which were upset that radio stations were taking away some of their advertising. They printed stories about a wide

Fort Dix was a gathering and training place for soldiers heading for or coming home from war.

panic to make it look like radio newscasts could not be trusted. The *New York Daily News* published a large headline that read: Fake Radio 'War' Stirs Terror Through U.S.

After World War II, many white people from Newark, Trenton, and other New Jersey cities began to move to surrounding areas, called suburbs. This shift was fueled by a boom in auto sales. To keep up with the growing number of vehicles on the road, New Jersey built two major roadways in the 1950s. Completed in 1951, the New Jersey Turnpike quickly became one of the busiest highways in the country. The Garden State Parkway connected the busy northern suburbs with resort areas along the Atlantic Coast.

As suburbs prospered, many cities in New Jersey began to crumble. Many African Americans either could not afford to move to other areas or were not allowed to move because of discrimination. Some manufacturing plants moved out of the cities as well, taking away jobs and tax revenues. City governments could not

The First Pitch

The first baseball game with rules similar to current ones was played in Hoboken, on Elysian Fields, on June 19, 1846.

maintain important services. Living conditions in cities got worse, and tension between blacks and whites increased. Riots broke out in Newark and other cities in the late 1960s.

New Jersey Today

After an economic slump in the mid 1990s, the urban areas of New Jersey began to recover. Along the Hudson River, decaying wharfs and empty warehouses were replaced by modern townhouses, apartment buildings, offices, and shopping malls. Rotting piers and junk heaps gave way to parks, small-boat harbors, and recreation areas. Dozens of New York City companies moved to these renewed areas.

New Jerseyans have fought over reducing the bad effects of industrialization and development and have worked to protect the environment. In 2007, the state passed a law requiring a 20 percent cut in greenhouses gas emissions by the year 2020. Greenhouse gases such as carbon dioxide contribute to global warming—the slow rise in worldwide temperatures. However, in 2011 Governor Chris Christie pulled the state out of the Regional Greenhouse Gas Initiative, a nine-state program designed to reduce greenhouse gas emissions. At that time, New Jersey's greenhouse gas emissions were already below the 2020 requirements. Governor Christie said the program was a tax on people who pay for energy in New Jersey. He wants to file lawsuits against polluters in neighboring states, saying they are responsible for most of New Jersey's air pollution. He also wants to prosecute businesses in New Jersey that fail to reduce pollution. Supporters of the initiative say it is good for the state and creates jobs.

The severe recession, or economic downturn, that hit the nation in 2008 had a strong impact on New Jersey. Businesses closed and many jobs were lost. By the summer of 2014, the economy of New Jersey was showing slow but continual expansion. Many private sector jobs had been added. However, the unemployment rate was still slightly above the national average.

Like all states, New Jersey will continue to face challenges. However, the recent revival of city areas and the success of preservation efforts offer hope that residents can

The northeastern section of New Jersey is heavily industrial.

continue to improve New Jersey's urban areas, while preserving garden areas and open spaces.

Another major contributor to economic difficulties in New Jersey was Hurricane Sandy, which devastated the New Jersey coastline in 2012, destroying homes, flooding businesses, and damaging key tourist attractions and boardwalks. New Jersey has since rebuilt many of the attractions, and the tourist industry is on its way back to full health. Ironically, the hurricane damage may lead to economic growth—billions of dollars had to be spent on new roads, new buildings, and new infrastructure, which meant that thousands of new jobs were created.

America's First Hollywood

In the early twentieth century, Fort Lee, New Jersey, was the movie capital of the world. From about 1907 to 1917, most of the biggest movies were made there. Many Wild West scenes were shot near the Palisades. Eventually moviemakers headed to Hollywood, California, where the weather and open spaces made filming much easier.

Hurricane Sandy, a superstorm, destroyed large sections of the Jersey shoreline.

10 KEY DATES IN STATE HISTORY

1. 1660
The Dutch establish a permanent settlement near present-day Jersey City.

2. December 18, 1787
New Jersey becomes the third state when it ratifies the U.S. Constitution. Nine of the original thirteen colonies had to ratify the document before it could go into effect. New Hampshire became the ninth state on June 21, 1788.

3. October 22, 1879
Thomas Edison invents the first workable light bulb. It had a filament of carbonized bamboo. Edison also designed a system to get electricity from power stations to bulbs in the house.

4. November 5, 1912
New Jersey governor Woodrow Wilson is elected president of the United States. He is reelected in 1916.

5. October 1, 1928
The airport now called Newark Liberty International Airport opens. At the time, it was the biggest airport in the world.

6. May 6, 1937
The airship *Hindenburg* crashes and burns at Lakehurst, apparently when a spark ignites the airship's hydrogen. Of the ninety passengers, thirty-five died.

7. November 30, 1951
The New Jersey Turnpike opens from its southern terminus to Woodbridge. The rest of the then 118-mile road was opened by January 1952.

8. November 2, 1993
Christine Todd Whitman is elected to be the first female governor of New Jersey.

9. September 11, 2001
Almost 700 New Jerseyans are killed in the terrorist attacks on the World Trade Center in New York City.

10. October 29, 2012
Hurricane Sandy hits the New Jersey coast, devastating homes and businesses, and leaving millions without power for weeks. Thirty-seven people were killed in New Jersey by the wind, rain, and flooding.

New Jersey has a dense and diverse population.

The People

The population of New Jersey exploded during the 1900s. The growth continued into the twenty-first century. The 2000 Census showed that New Jersey's population had grown almost 9 percent in ten years—from 7.7 million people in 1990 to 8.4 million in 2000. In 2010, the population was estimated at close to nine million. New Jersey—already the most crowded state in the nation—was becoming even more crowded. But the population is spread around unevenly. The southern part of the state still has wide-open stretches of farms, forests, and marshland.

Coming to New Jersey

Over the past few centuries, New Jersey's population has undergone changes similar to those in other parts of the Northeast. More than three-quarters of the colonists in New Jersey in the 1700s could trace their origins to Great Britain and Ireland. The same was true of the people in New York and the New England colonies. Many Dutch and Swedish settlers and their descendants also made New Jersey their home.

After 1800, shiploads of immigrants from Europe arrived at New Jersey ports and other ports throughout the Northeast. In the 1840s, the numbers of immigrants increased dramatically, especially from Ireland and Germany. In Ireland, a blight, or disease, struck

Immigrants had to pass through Ellis Island before taking a ferry to the mainland.

the potato crop. Potatoes were the major source of food and income for many people. The countryside was devastated, and more than a million people lost their lives. Others escaped the famine on ships bound for the United States. During the same period, large numbers of German immigrants fled from the political problems in their homeland to start new lives in the United States.

Many of the new immigrants headed for New Jersey cities, hoping to find factory jobs. They often met angry opposition from native-born Americans. Some people disliked the newcomers' unfamiliar customs and were afraid that immigrants would take jobs away from them. Gradually, the newcomers overcame the prejudice and fear. Many young Irish women found jobs as household servants. Some German families opened restaurants, butcher shops, and "beer gardens." Other immigrants worked in factories, hospitals, and stores. Many became firefighters or police officers or joined the clergy. Some pursued higher education. Despite limited opportunities, the immigrants became lawyers, doctors, writers, and teachers. Some eventually became active in politics.

The 1880s started a new period of immigration. More people were coming to the United States than ever before. Many arrived from other parts of Europe, such as Russia and what is now Poland. Large numbers of immigrants from Italy settled in New Jersey. The state's population continued to increase through the 1900s.

A Changing Population

Since the early 1970s, New Jersey's population has become even more diverse. Changes in the nation's immigration laws led to an increase in new arrivals from regions other than Europe. In recent decades, people from Spanish-speaking countries in Latin America and people from Asian countries have come to New Jersey in larger numbers than before.

Hispanics, such as this family from Passaic, form the largest minority group in New Jersey.

10 KEY PEOPLE

Buzz Aldrin

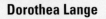

Justice Samuel Alito

Dorothea Lange

1. Edwin "Buzz" Aldrin

Born in Montclair in 1930, this decorated fighter pilot and astronaut's 1966 spacewalk was the longest and most successful at that time. On July 20, 1969, Aldrin became only the second person to set foot on the moon.

2. Samuel Alito

Born in Trenton, New Jersey in 1950, he served as U.S. Attorney in New Jersey, and was nominated by George H.W. Bush to the U.S. Court of Appeals for the Third Circuit in 1990. In 2005, Bush nominated Alito to the Supreme Court, and he took office in 2006.

3. Thomas Edison

Born in 1847 in Ohio and raised in Michigan, Edison spent most of his life in New Jersey. He turned out more than a thousand inventions, including the phonograph and the first long-lasting electric light bulb. Edison, New Jersey, is named in his honor.

4. F. Scott Fitzgerald

Fitzgerald attended high school and Princeton University in New Jersey. He is best known for his novel *The Great Gatsby*. Fitzgerald coined the term "the Jazz Age" to describe the 1920s in the U.S.

5. Dorothea Lange

Born in Hoboken in 1895, Lange was a world-famous photographer who used her skills to help people. During the Great Depression of the 1930s, her vivid photographs called attention to the harsh lives of many people in those years.

NEW JERSEY

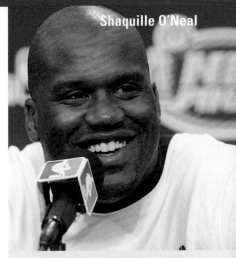
Shaquille O'Neal

6. Jack Nicholson

Nicholson is one of the most critically acclaimed actors in Hollywood history. He grew up in Neptune City, New Jersey, and moved to California after high school. Nicholson has earned nineteen Academy Award nominations, and won twice.

7. Shaquille O'Neal

The man known as "Shaq" was born in 1972 in Newark. O'Neal spent nineteen years playing in the NBA and won four championships. He has released several rap albums, acted in major motion pictures, and appeared in ad campaigns.

8. Queen Latifah

Born Dana Elaine Owens in Newark on March 18, 1970, Latifah earned a Grammy Award in 1995 for Best Rap Solo Performance. She received an Academy Award nomination for her role in *Chicago*, and won Screen Actors Guild awards and a Golden Globe award.

Queen Latifah

9. Bruce Springsteen

Bruce Springsteen was born in 1949 in Freehold, a mill town in Monmouth County. One of the biggest rock musicians of the 1970s and 1980s, his music often reflects the lives of everyday working people.

10. Meryl Streep

Raised in Bernardsville, Meryl Streep has received fifteen Oscar nominations, won three Academy Awards, two Emmy Awards, and eight Golden Globes. Among her films are *Doubt*, *The Devil Wears Prada*, *The Bridges of Madison County*, and *Sophie's Choice*.

Bruce Springsteen

Who New Jerseyans Are

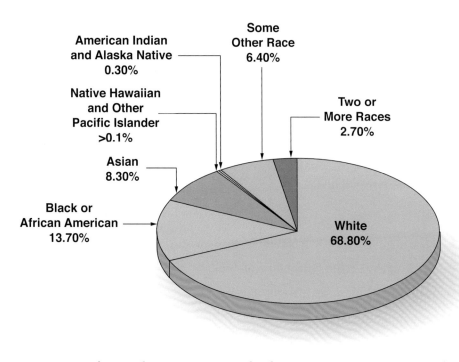

American Indian and Alaska Native 0.30%

Native Hawaiian and Other Pacific Islander >0.1%

Asian 8.30%

Black or African American 13.70%

Some Other Race 6.40%

Two or More Races 2.70%

White 68.80%

Total Population 8,791,894

Hispanic or Latino (of any race):
- 1,555,144 people (17.70%)

Note: The pie chart shows the racial breakdown of the state's population based on the categories used by the U.S. Bureau of the Census. The Census Bureau reports information for Hispanics or Latinos separately, since they may be of any race. Percentages in the pie chart may not add to 100 because of rounding.

Source: U.S. Bureau of the Census, 2010 Census

New Jersey's population is constantly changing. Between 2010 and 2013, the Hispanic and Asian populations each increased by at least 5 percent. Two out of five Asians in New Jersey have roots in India. Asian Indians are the fastest-growing immigrant group in the state. The next-largest groups of Asian immigrants are people from China, the Philippines, and Korea.

Also, the number of "Baby Boomers" (those people born during the years following World War II) who are between the ages of 60 and 69 increased by more than 6.5 percent. New Jersey is becoming more ethnically diverse, and older.

Hispanics are the largest minority group in New Jersey. They make up more than one-sixth of the state's population, and their numbers are growing. Half of the Hispanics in the state are under the age of thirty.

Almost half the state's Hispanic people are foreign-born. Many struggle to find jobs, especially in hard times, or earn low wages for hard work. However, increasing numbers of Hispanics are business owners and professionals.

The influence of many different immigrant cultures can be seen across New Jersey. Large communities of people from the same ethnic group can be found in cities across the state. Restaurants and other businesses that sell food and goods from abroad are very popular. A walk down a main street in Hoboken or neighboring Jersey City can reveal a worldwide sampling of shops and restaurants—Brazilian, Cuban, South African, Chinese,

Greek, and Sicilian. Additionally, many cultural events and festivals celebrating the heritage of different ethnic groups are held throughout the state.

African Americans in New Jersey

In the 1800s, African Americans made up only a small portion of New Jersey's population. As slavery in the state came to an end, free African Americans worked at different types of jobs. A few owned farms, and a larger number worked as farm laborers. Even after the Civil War ended, life was often hard for them. Jobs were scarce, and prejudice was widespread.

The United States fought in World Wars I and II in the first half of the twentieth century. New Jersey's factories and shipyards had to quickly manufacture the weapons and equipment needed by America's military forces. Thousands of African Americans moved north from southern states to find work. Many African Americans found jobs as laborers. Over the years, others became scholars, doctors, lawyers, teachers, business owners, and entertainers.

For twenty years after the end of World War II in 1945, many people

In Their Own Words

"Cynicism cripples our imagination and limits our ability to see faint possibilities amidst glaring problems."

–Former Newark mayor Cory Booker

A community leader pleads for calm during the riots in Newark.

African Americans make up about one-seventh of the state's population.

moved to growing New Jersey suburbs, leaving the crowded, congested cities behind. Few African American families could afford such a move, and white people and real estate agencies in suburbs would often not rent or sell homes to African Americans. Most cities and suburbs were segregated, meaning that black families could find housing only in black neighborhoods.

The frustrations of African Americans increased during the civil rights movement of the 1950s and 1960s. The Rev. Dr. Martin Luther King, Jr. led protest marches through the South. He and other civil rights leaders helped force Southern cities and states to remove laws that discriminated against African Americans. Racial tensions existed in Northern states,

Late End for Slavery in New Jersey

There were 2,909 black men from New Jersey who served in the Union Army during the Civil War, and yet slavery was not officially abolished in the state until 1866, after the war, when the thirteenth Amendment to the Constitution was passed. At that time, the last sixteen slaves in the state were freed.

too. In the late 1960s, race riots broke out in northern cities. One of the worst riots occurred in Newark in July 1967. Twenty-six people were killed, and more than one thousand were wounded. Rioters caused more than $10 million in property damage.

Like other northern states, New Jersey launched programs to try to modernize cities and create more opportunities for African Americans. More housing for low-income people was built. New state colleges had lower tuition fees, making them more affordable to New Jerseyans from all walks of life. A commuter railroad improved transportation, and job training programs were established.

Today, African Americans make up about one-seventh of the state's population and are very active in the politics, education, and businesses of the state.

Living in New Jersey

Why do people live in New Jersey? That is a question with many answers. Many move to the state because of the job opportunities it offers. Large corporations have been based in New Jersey for a long time. Recently, more corporate offices and research companies have moved out of New York City to New Jersey to take advantage of greater space, lower rents, and lower taxes. These businesses create jobs in factories, offices, and stores.

New Jersey's location is attractive to commuters. Many New Jerseyans live in suburbs outside cities where they work. People call these suburbs "bedroom communities"—places where city workers sleep. Several bridges and tunnels cross the Hudson River to New York City, and bridges span the Delaware River to Philadelphia. Commuters can travel by train, bus, or car, and some can conveniently cross the Hudson River by ferry. Highways may be crowded and trips may be long, but for many commuters, living in New Jersey is worth the trouble.

Other residents enjoy the quiet, country life offered by farmland in the south. The shoreline is popular with people who enjoy the ocean and beaches. Many people are drawn to New Jersey by its schools. Some New Jersey schools are among the highest-rated in the nation. In the 2014 U.S. News Best High School rankings, twenty-five New Jersey schools earned gold medals, including Biotechnology High School of Freehold. It was ranked number 11 in the country. New Jersey is also home to fine universities and colleges that attract students from across the country and around the world.

Like all states, New Jersey is not perfect. Poverty and crime are problems in some areas. However, to most of the state's ever-changing population, living in New Jersey has many benefits.

1. Annual Shad Festival

Every spring, the shad, a type of fish, start their run up the Delaware River to spawn. The shad run is an exciting time for people who like to fish or just enjoy the once-a-year fish feast in Lambertville.

2. Battle of Monmouth

In late June, hundreds of people in period costume re-create the American Revolution battle at Monmouth. The actors use muskets and other authentic equipment to help show how General Washington saved the day for the Americans.

3. Cranberry Festival

The Cranberry Festival is held in Chatsworth in October. It celebrates cranberries—an important crop in the state—and shows off many ways to use them. There are activities such as live music, a classic automobile show, and many artists and craftsmen display their work.

4. Hummingbird Extravaganza

The Hummingbird Extravaganza is held in Swainton in August. The popular event provides demonstrations of how to attract these tiny birds to backyard gardens.

5. New Jersey State Fair/Sussex County Farm and Horse Show

The state fair and horse show is a big event in the middle of the summer. It is held at the Sussex County Fairgrounds in Augusta. Highlights include everything from fruit and vegetable competitions and racing pigs to wood-chopping contests and carnival rides.

Shad Festival

Cranberry Festival

NEW JERSEY

6. New Jersey Festival of Ballooning

Each July, dozens of colorful hot air balloons brighten the skies above Readington in the north-central part of the state. Balloon enthusiasts come from all parts of the country. There are fireworks and performances by top entertainers.

7. Reenactment of Washington's Crossing of the Delaware

This event re-creates Washington's famous crossing on Christmas night 1776, which was followed by the victory of the Continental Army at the Battle of Trenton. It is meant to be an annual event, but sometimes the current is too strong for the actors to safely cross the river.

8. Super Science Weekend

Held early in the year at the State Museum in Trenton, the Super Science Weekend features exhibits and hands-on activities for kids of all ages. Among the exhibits are a planetarium and an innovation lab.

9. Victorian Week in Cape May

Cape May is noted for its many old-fashioned houses and inns from the time of Britain's Queen Victoria (1837–1901). Visitors can tour these remarkable buildings and enjoy other events during this ten-day celebration in October.

10. Wildwood International Kite Festival

Kite builders and competitors from as far away as Japan come to Wildwood on Memorial Day weekend to show off many kinds of colorful kites. Part of the country's largest kite festival takes place on the beach.

Festival of Ballooning

Victorian Week

The executive and legislative branches, as well as other governmental agencies, have offices in the New Jersey State House.

How the Government Works

Every state has different layers of government. From the smallest village to the largest city, nearly every community has a government. There are more than five hundred of these communities—or municipalities—in New Jersey. These include cities, towns, townships, boroughs, and villages. Most cities are governed by a mayor and a city council. There are many other local bodies with important powers, such as school boards, planning boards, zoning boards, and water commissions.

Cities, towns, and townships are grouped together to form counties. New Jersey has twenty-one counties. They are governed by groups called boards of chosen freeholders. This term dates back to colonial times, when only men who owned property, called freeholders, could vote or hold office. The counties handle a wide variety of responsibilities, involving schools, roads, hospitals, and other key areas.

The next level is state government. The governor, the governor's staff, the legislature, and the judicial system work together to create and uphold laws and run the government. New Jersey has a large degree of "home rule," which means that under the state's constitution and laws, local governments have more power than they do in many other states.

The official residence of the governor is called Drumthwacket, and is located in Princeton.

As of 2014, New Jersey had fourteen representatives in the U.S. Congress in Washington, D.C. Voters in New Jersey elected twelve members to the U.S. House of Representatives. Like voters in all other states, they also elect two U.S. senators.

Branches of Government

EXECUTIVE

For a long time, New Jersey was one of the few states that had no lieutenant governor. The lieutenant governor is like the vice president of the state. In 2001 and again in 2004, the governor of New Jersey resigned and was replaced by the person who was president of the senate. Then, in November 2005, New Jersey voters approved an amendment to the constitution that created the position of lieutenant governor. Starting in 2009, the lieutenant governor runs for office on the same ticket with the governor. The lieutenant governor takes over if the governor resigns or dies in office. The governor and lieutenant governor are elected to four-year terms. Other officials such as the attorney general, secretary of state, and treasurer, are appointed by the governor.

LEGISLATIVE

The legislature is made up of two houses: the senate and the general assembly. The senate has forty members, and the general assembly has eighty. Members of the assembly are elected every two years. Senators serve four-year terms, except the first term of a new decade, which is only two years.

JUDICIAL

The court system has several divisions. Municipal courts hear cases for minor offenses, such as traffic tickets and shoplifting. Municipal judges are appointed by the local government. Each county has a superior court, which hears cases involving criminal, civil, and family law. People who do not agree with the outcome of their case can have it reviewed by an appellate court. New Jersey also has a tax court. The supreme court is the highest court in the state and hears the most important cases. Judges for the superior, tax, and supreme courts are selected by the governor and must be approved by the state senate. Each of these judge's term is seven years.

How a Bill Becomes a Law

Ideas for new state laws often come from concerned citizens, but any proposed law, called a bill, must be officially submitted by an assembly member or a senator. A committee studies the bill and may **amend**, or change, it. Committees have public meetings where people from the community may speak about the bill. If the committee approves it, the bill is then debated in the house in which it was first proposed. Legislators may argue about the bill and amend it further. A bill passes if it receives a majority of the vote—twenty-one votes if it is in the senate, or forty-one if it is in the general assembly. If enough members of one house vote for the bill, it is sent to the other house, where it goes through a similar process. If the second house approves the bill, it goes on to the governor. The governor can approve the bill or may decide to **veto**, or reject, it. If the governor does not take any action on the bill, it can become a law. If the governor vetoes the bill, it can still become law if two-thirds of both the senate and the general assembly vote for it.

It's Illegal to Pump Your Own Gas

Since 1949, it has been illegal for a driver to pump gas in New Jersey; gas must be pumped by the gas station owner or attendant. Other states also require full service gas stations, but only two—Oregon and New Jersey—ban self-service stations.

Union City High School provides educational opportunitities for a student body that is largely Hispanic.

Both legislative houses can also propose amendments to the state constitution. If three-fifths of the assembly and the senate approve the amendment, it goes on the ballot in the next general election. The amendment passes if the majority of voters approve it. The current state constitution has been amended more than thirty times.

Court Ordered

One major change in New Jersey's laws came about because of a ruling made by the state Supreme Court. The court ruled in 1973 that funding schools through property taxes discriminated against the poor. The thought was that property values in poor neighborhoods were lower, so there would be less tax money to pay for education.

Three years later the court shut down the state's public schools for eight days because the government had not devised a way to fund schools equally. That resulted in the state enacting its first income tax in 1976. Tax rates of 2 percent for people with the lowest incomes to 2.5 percent were established. Those rates have been amended many times.

There have been numerous lawsuits over this issue since the first court ruling. However, a lot of progress has been made. In 2004, the Education Trust in Washington, D.C., issued a report that named New Jersey a leader in equal school funding for poor and minority students.

New Jersey Politics

New Jersey's strong emphasis on home rule has encouraged many citizens to make their views known to local and state officials. Citizens may also run for many types of local office. Many of these positions are unpaid, but they offer the person a role in making decisions that affect the community. However, some people say that New Jersey has too many local bodies that have too much power. Over the years, New Jersey officials have sometimes abused these powers. Some were convicted of accepting bribes in return for granting contracts or giving favorable treatment to certain businesses.

New Jersey has a majority of Democrat voters who usually elect a majority Democrat senate and house. In 2010, Christopher "Chris" Christie, a Republican, took over as governor. Governor Christie came under fire from conservatives for meeting with President Barack Obama to show him the damage caused by Hurricane Sandy. He delivered the keynote speech at the Republican National Convention in 2012.

In Their Own Words

"I'm a...good Republican. And a good conservative Republican ... but that does not mean I would ever put party before my state or party before my country."

—New Jersey governor Chris Christie

Governor Chris Christie delivers the keynote speech at the 2012 Republican National Convention.

Cory Booker: Mayor of Newark, 2006-2013

Born in 1969, Booker grew up in Harrington Park, and is active in helping less-fortunate, low-income people in Newark's inner city. He was elected to the city council in 1998, and elected mayor in 2006. He moved on to the United States Senate in 2013.

Bill Bradley: United States Senator, 1979-1997

Bradley, a Princeton graduate, earned an Olympic Gold Medal in 1964 prior to starting his outstanding career with the NBA's New York Knicks. As a U.S. senator, he took part in overhauling the tax code in 1986. He ran for president in 1999, but lost the Democratic nomination to Al Gore.

Woodrow Wilson: President of the United States, 1913-1921

Woodrow Wilson served as governor of New Jersey before being elected the twenty-eighth U.S. president. He guided the country through World War I and won a Nobel Peace Prize for helping to negotiate the treaty to end the war, which included a plan for the League of Nations.

NEW JERSEY
YOU CAN MAKE A DIFFERENCE

Contact Lawmakers

Contacting your local legislator—senator or house representative—can make a big difference. If there is an issue that you feel passionate about changing, make a list of clear arguments that you can present to your legislator when you contact them.

To contact New Jersey state legislators, visit:

www.njleg.state.nj.us/members/legsearch.asp

Click on the Interactive Map of Legislative Districts, and then click on the area in which you live. You will find contact information for your state representatives.

To contact your national representatives, visit:

www.govtrack.us/congress/members/NJ

Click on your representative and then on their official website for contact information.

To view your county and municipal websites, visit:

www.state.nj.us/nj/gov/county/localgov.html

What You Can Do

New Jersey lawmakers have made many decisions of importance to people in the state. Some of them have been controversial, such as the 1978 law to permit gambling in Atlantic City.

Other measures have been less controversial. For example, in 2010, the state amended its crosswalk law aimed at reducing the number of pedestrians killed in traffic accidents. The law requires drivers to come to a full stop whenever a pedestrian begins to cross a street at a crosswalk. It also increases the penalty for "jaywalking," or crossing a street when and where it is not allowed. New Jersey has the highest pedestrian fatality rate in the country.

Before 2010, New Jersey's crosswalk law hadn't been altered in fifty years. The impetus for the change was the death of Casey Feldman, a twenty-one-year-old who was struck and killed in a crosswalk in Ocean City in 2009 by a distracted driver.

New Jersey is a leader in
cranberry production.

Making a Living

5

New Jersey's economy is as diverse as its population. Fields such as agriculture, research, manufacturing, service, and tourism bring money into the state and provide jobs for its residents.

Agriculture

Much of New Jersey is covered with cities and suburbs, and large areas are protected for wetlands or wildlife preserves. Yet close to 20 percent of the land area is still devoted to farmland.

There are about ten thousand farms in the state. Most are fairly small and family-owned. Prosperous dairy farms and orchards cover the hillsides of the northwestern corner of the state. In the northeastern corner of New Jersey, greenhouses and nurseries produce many types of colorful flowers. Many flowers grown there end up in New York City markets. On the level lands just north of the Pine Barrens, truck farms produce a variety of vegetables, especially tomatoes, sweet corn, lettuce, and beans. New Jersey's Pine Barrens is home to the largest cranberry bogs outside New England. New Jersey is also one of the top blueberry-growing states.

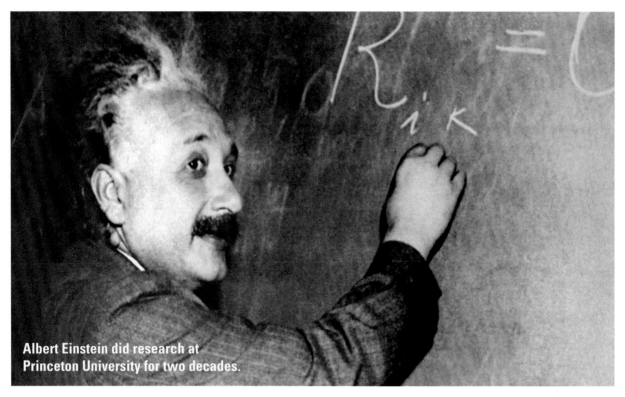

Albert Einstein did research at Princeton University for two decades.

Although fishing is not a major New Jersey industry, the long coast is an excellent source of clams. The coastal waters are also good for catching flounder, lobsters, and oysters.

Research

New Jersey is known as the state where the famed inventor Thomas Alva Edison had his laboratories. The state is also the home of the Institute for Advanced Study in Princeton, where the scientific genius Albert Einstein did research from the mid 1930s to the mid 1950s.

Other well-known research organizations with facilities in New Jersey include Bell Laboratories and Western Electric. Many drug companies, computer companies, and aerospace research firms are also based in the state. The large **pharmaceutical** and health care products company Johnson & Johnson has its headquarters in New Brunswick, as well as research centers and offices elsewhere in the state.

Manufacturing

New Jersey has a long industrial history. The state has been a leader in industrial development since the mid 1800s. Smoke once hung over the cities as machines churned out an incredible variety of products in large quantities—shoes, machine parts, chemicals, furniture, and dozens of other items. During both world wars, New Jersey turned its industrial might to the production of weapons and ammunition. The state has been losing manufacturing jobs in recent years, but some areas are growing. Manufacturing jobs in the state often require special skills, and they usually pay well.

Today, New Jersey is the national leader in making drugs and other medical products, its biggest manufacturing industry. The related field of **biotechnology** has become a key industry, too. Biotechnology is the use of biological materials and processes to make useful products, such as pharmaceuticals.

Another big area is the production of chemicals, including such household products as cleansers, soaps, and shampoos. Computer and electronic products have grown in importance. New Jersey is also one of the top states in food processing, including freezing and canning foods and producing wholesale baked goods.

Twenty-Four Hour Food

Many sources claim that New Jersey has the highest number of diners per capita of any state in the U.S., and many of those diners are open twenty-four hours a day. New Jersey is often referred to as the "Diner Capital of the World."

At Your Service

Like that of other states, New Jersey's economy has become increasingly geared toward service industries. About three of every five New Jersey workers has a job in this sector. Service industries include transportation, education, health care, banking, and insurance. People who work in retail stores, restaurants, and hotels are also part of the service industry.

Shipping

The Port of New York and New Jersey is the largest port on the East Coast and third-largest in the United States (behind the ports in Houston, Texas, and in southern Louisiana). Major port facilities, operated by the Port Authority of New York and New Jersey, are located in Newark, Elizabeth, and Jersey City, as well as in New York City. In 2010, more than $175 billion worth of cargo entered or left the United States through the Port of New York and New Jersey. The port provides jobs for thousands of New Jersey workers.

Tourism

Throughout the state's history, people have visited New Jersey to enjoy all it has to offer. Today, tourist activities bring in close to $40 billion in revenue each year, and tourism provides jobs for one in nine New Jersey workers.

In 1934, during the Great Depression, Charles Darrow, an out-of-work salesman, sold a game he called Monopoly to the Parker Brothers game company. The properties on the

Cranberries

Nuclear Energy

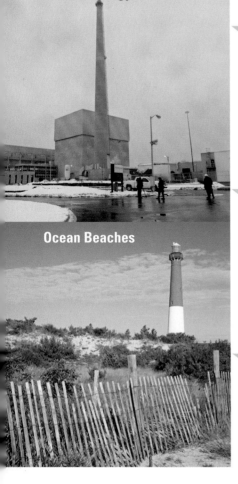

Ocean Beaches

1. Blueberries

Not only does New Jersey produce millions of pounds of blueberries every year—making it between third and fifth in state blueberry production annually—but farms where you can pick your own blueberries are an important part of **agri-tourism** in the state.

2. Cranberries

New Jersey is one of the nation's leading producers of cranberries. The cranberry bogs are located in the northern part of the Interior Coastal Plain.

3. Greenhouses and Nurseries

Products grown in nurseries and greenhouses provide the largest portion of the state's agricultural income. Nurseries produce a wide variety of shrubs, such as juniper and holly. Greenhouses provide New York City markets with roses, geraniums, lilies, orchids, and poinsettias.

4. Nuclear Energy

Oyster Creek Nuclear Generating Station is the oldest nuclear power plant still operating in the United States, coming online in 1969. New Jersey has three nuclear plants that generate most of its electricity, which means that the state is ranked very low in its greenhouse gas emissions.

5. Ocean Beaches

Sandy beaches and barrier islands stretch for about 130 miles (200 km) along the Atlantic Coast. Two of the state's greatest natural resources are its state parks at Sandy Hook in the north and Island Beach in the south.

NEW JERSEY

6. Pharmaceuticals

A center for drug research, manufacturing, and sales, some of the state's big drug makers have recently merged with out-of-state companies. Factories have closed and jobs have been lost. At the same time, many small **biotechnology** research companies have sprung up.

Pharmaceuticals

7. Satellites

The state's research laboratories have played a key role in developing modern telecommunications. The first satellite used for weather observation was developed in New Jersey in 1960, as well as the first satellite used to beam live pictures between the United States and Europe.

8. Solar Energy

New Jersey ranks second in the nation in the number of solar power installations, and is second in the nation in the number of jobs it has created in the solar power industry (in 2013, about 6,500 jobs).

Solar Energy

9. Tourism and Gambling

Atlantic City has become one of the most popular gambling destinations in the country. Resorts, gambling, and tourism industries made more than $40 billion in 2013, a record year.

10. Transportation

New Jersey has one of the busiest, most modern transportation systems in the world. Hundreds of millions of vehicles travel each year on the now 148-mile-long (238 km) New Jersey Turnpike. Newark Liberty International Airport is one of the busiest airports in the country.

Transportation

Recipe for New Jersey Blueberry Cobbler

In honor of one of New Jersey's biggest agricultural products, here is a recipe for blueberry cobbler. This tasty, simple dessert is sure to please, and you can tell your family all about New Jersey's world renowned blueberry industry!

What You Need

1 1/4 cups (296 grams) all-purpose flour

1/2 cup (118 g) sugar

1/4 teaspoon (1.25 milliliters) salt

1 1/2 teaspoons (7 mL) baking powder

3/4 cup (117 mL) whole milk

1/3 cup (78 mL) butter, melted

2 cups (473 g) fresh blueberries

1/3 (71 g) cup sugar

1 teaspoon (5 mL) vanilla extract

What to Do

• Add flour, 1/2 cup (118 g) sugar, salt, and baking powder to a mixing bowl; stir to combine.

• Add in milk and butter; stir to combine.

• Spread batter into a greased 8-inch (20 cm) square baking pan.

• Sprinkle blueberries evenly over batter.

• Sprinkle with 1/3 cup (71 g) sugar and drizzle with vanilla.

• Bake at 350°F (177°C) for 40–45 minutes or until a pick comes out clean.

• Serve plain or with ice cream on top.

board were all named after real streets in Atlantic City. Although many people say Darrow did not invent the game himself, he helped make it one of the most successful board games in history. Today, at the real corner of Boardwalk and Park Place, a brass plaque honors Darrow for his achievement.

Tourism got a big boost after casino gambling became legal in Atlantic City in 1978. The city's hotels and famous boardwalk had made it a popular vacation spot for a hundred years, but it had been in decline in recent decades. Once gambling was permitted, developers and investors moved in to create glittering resorts that rivaled those in Las Vegas. By 2014, competition from new casinos in neighboring states hurt business in Atlanta City, leading to the closing of four of its eleven casinos. However, there is more to Atlantic City than gambling. Families go to see shows, stroll along the boardwalk, and enjoy the sun and sand of the beaches. There are many free events, such as outdoor concerts and light shows. About twenty-seven million guests now visit the city each year.

People visit New Jersey's cities to attend plays, movies, and concerts. The state's museums are widely respected. The state has a battleship museum, an agricultural museum, and many historical museums and historical sites. Of course, the Garden State also has many beautiful public gardens.

The boardwalk in Atlantic City provides many thrills.

The Liberty Science Center in Jersey City features exhibits and hands-on activities, as well as educational programs for students. The center is located in Liberty State Park, on the western shore of Upper New York Bay. Ferries from Liberty State Park take visitors to the Statue of Liberty and to Ellis Island.

The Jersey Shore continues to draw millions of visitors each summer. From Sandy Hook in the north to Cape May at the state's southern tip, visitors come to splash in the waves and lounge on the beach. Over the years, resorts and businesses that cater to shore visitors have brought in big money for the state.

Sports fans have plenty to cheer about in New Jersey. The New Jersey Devils, the state's pro hockey team, play at the Prudential Center in Newark. The Jets and the Giants football teams may represent New York, but they play their home games at the $1.6-billion stadium at the Meadowlands constructed in 2010. The Meadowlands is also home to one of three major horse racing tracks in the state.

Challenging Times

New Jersey—along with the rest of the country—struggled through difficult economic times in the early 1990s. Many people were unemployed, and government studies showed an increase in poverty levels. The economy began to recover in 1993.

Children take advantage of hands-on activities at the Liberty Science Center in Jersey City.

New Jersey suffered again from a severe economic downturn that began in the United States in late 2007 and grew much worse the next year. By the end of 2009, nearly 10 percent of New Jersey's workforce was unemployed. Things had improved by May 2014, when the rate fell to 6.9 percent.

Balancing the Economy and the Environment

Throughout most of the 1900s, New Jersey's factories produced a wealth of products, but they also created gloomy clouds of smog. Rivers and lakes were polluted with chemicals and waste.

In the last part of the century, the state made progress in cleaning up rivers and streams. Abandoned factories and shipyards were replaced with modern housing and recreation areas. Special attention was also paid to the state's native plants and animals. State lawmakers introduced strict rules regarding pollution and land development.

Private organizations such as the Nature Conservancy and the New Jersey Audubon Society have helped promote policies that save open spaces. In 1978, for example, the Pinelands National Reserve was established to limit development and protect the environment. The reserve covers 1,700 square miles (4,400 sq km) of the Atlantic Coastal Plain. This large area was the country's first national reserve. Much of it is forested land that can be reached only by foot.

One bold plan involved the development and protection of the Hackensack Meadows, commonly known as the Meadowlands. This region of marshlands and ponds was created by the last ice age. Different agencies manage the land and try to protect native plants and animals and control pollution. The land has also been used to develop a unique area that includes major sports and entertainment facilities. The Meadowlands area is an example of how New Jersey's residents and agencies can work together to protect the land while also finding ways to help the economy.

As New Jersey continues to grow, the effort to balance economic growth with environmental protection will be an ongoing challenge for the Garden State.

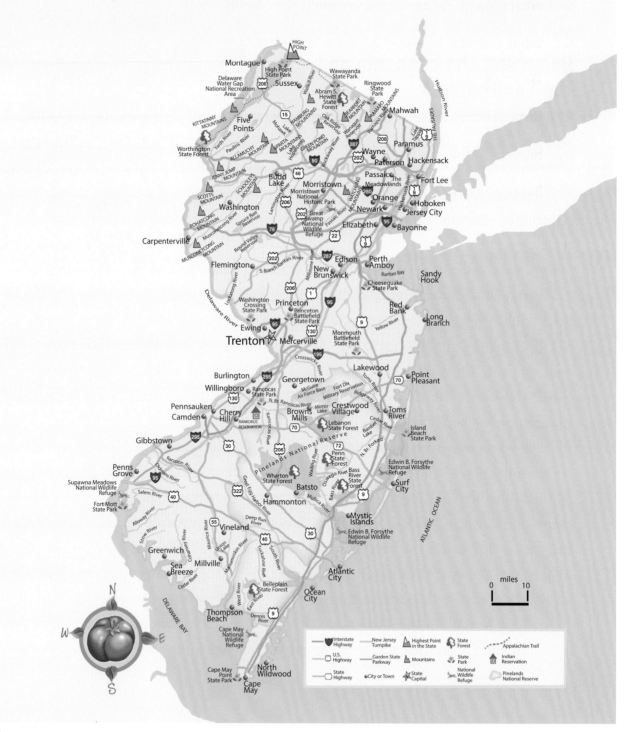

NEW JERSEY

MAP SKILLS

1. What is the northernmost city or town in New Jersey?

2. Estimate the distance in miles of the widest part of the state.

3. Which highway runs the entire length of the state?

4. Name the three towns or cities closest to the capital.

5. Name two of the rivers that empty into the Delaware Bay.

6. Based on your estimation, which state forest has the largest area?

7. Which bodies of water border the state?

8. In which region is New Jersey the most mountainous?

9. Which city or town has a state park *and* a national wildlife refuge named after it?

10. What is the westernmost state park?

Wharton State Forest

Princeton University

10. Fort Mott State Park
9. Cape May
8. In the north
7. Delaware River, Hudson River, Delaware Bay, Atlantic Ocean
6. Worthington or Wharton State Forest
5. Among them are the Alloway, Stow, Cohansey, Cedar, Dennis, Maurice, Manumuskin, West, and East
4. Ewing, Princeton, and Mercerville
3. Garden State Parkway, or Interstate 95
2. Seventy miles between Penns Grove and Surf City
1. Montague

State Flag, Seal, and Song

The New Jersey state flag has the official state seal against a yellow background. The state seal shows two women standing on opposite sides of a shield. The shield has three plows, which represent agriculture. The woman to the left of the shield represents liberty. The woman to the right of the shield represents agriculture. Below the women and the shield are the words "Liberty and Prosperity" and "1776," the year of independence.

New Jersey is the only state without an official state song. Several songs have been nominated, but legal battles have stopped the process of actually signing the proposals into law. The song "I'm From New Jersey" was passed as the state song by both legislative houses in 1972, but the governor never signed it into law and nothing has changed since. To see the lyrics of that song, visit:

www.50states.com/songs/newjerse.htm#.U5nzt6XqKhM

Glossary

agricultural shifting A farming technique used by the Native Americans that rotated farms among locations.

agri-tourism Visiting a place for the purpose of exploring its agricultural settings, like touring vineyards and farms.

amend To change, often related to a constitution or legal document.

biotechnology The use of biological materials and processes to make useful products, such as pharmaceuticals.

matrilineal The family line based on motherhood.

monopoly A company that controls so much of an industry that it has no competition and can charge high prices.

nomadic A way of life characterized by moving frequently from place to place.

pharmaceutical Related to the production and development of medicine or drugs.

Prohibition The period from 1919 to 1933 in the United States when the Constitution was amended to ban the sale of alcohol.

sedentary Staying or living in one place instead of moving.

stagecoach An enclosed horse-drawn carriage, often used to carry people and mail.

suspension bridge A bridge in which the deck is hung below suspension cables that run between vertical towers.

turnpike A highway on which a toll is charged at intervals.

veto The right to reject a decision made by legislators.

watershed An area of land that divides water flowing to two different rivers.

More About New Jersey

BOOKS

Brunelli, Carol. *Woodrow Wilson*. Mankato, MN: The Child's World, 2009.

Freeberg, Ernest. *The Age of Edison: Electric Light and the Invention of Modern America*. New York, NY: Penguin Books, 2014.

Mazzella, Scott, and Steve Warren. *Hurricane Sandy: Long Beach Island and the Greatest Storm of the Jersey Shore*. West Creek, NJ: Down the Shore Publishing, 2013.

Nobleman, Marc Tyler. *The Hindenburg*. Mankato, MN: Compass Point Books, 2006.

WEBSITES

New Jersey News and Sports
www.nj.com

New Jersey Tourism
www.visitnj.org

The Official State of New Jersey Website
www.state.nj.us

ABOUT THE AUTHORs

David C. King is an award-winning author who has written more than forty books for children and young adults.

William McGeveran is a reference book editor and was editorial director at World Almanac Books.

Greg Clinton has taught literature, philosophy, and cultural studies at the middle and high school as well as undergraduate levels.

Index

Index